MW00426329

ANIMALS
OF THE
NIGHT

ANIMALS
OF THE
NIGHT

MERRY BANKS

PICTURES BY
RONALD HIMLER

CHARLES SCRIBNER'S SONS · NEW YORK

For Jim

— M. B.

Text copyright © 1990 by Merry Banks
Illustrations copyright © 1990 by Ronald Himler

Charles Scribner's Sons Books for Young Readers
Macmillan Publishing Company
866 Third Avenue, New York, NY 10022
Collier Macmillan Canada, Inc.

Printed in Hong Kong
10 9 8 7 6 5 4 3 2

Library of Congress Cataloging-in-Publication Data
Banks, Merry.   Animals of the night / Merry Banks;
pictures by Ronald Himler. — 1st ed.   p.   cm.
Summary: Describes in simple text and illustrations the
various animals that are active only at night.
1. Nocturnal animals — Juvenile literature.   [1. Nocturnal animals.]
I. Himler, Ronald, ill.   II. Title.
QL755.5.B28   1990   599'.051 — dc19   89–6194   CIP   AC
ISBN 0–684–19093–1

The sun sets.

The stars appear.

Sleepy children go to bed.

The moon shines down on the earth.

Flickering fireflies begin to dance. The crickets chirp
and a chorus of bullfrogs join in.

It is time for the night animals to come out from the
cool, dark places where they sleep during the day.

The owl soars through the sky in silent flight. His thick, soft feathers help him to glide through the air without

making a sound. He perches on a limb and watches the other animals of the night.

Out come the raccoons, looking for berries to eat.

With their small hands they search for food and wash it in
the stream. They eat, then scamper across the woods to play.

The armadillos march along the river banks, stopping
to dig for roots to eat.

To cross a small stream, they hold their breath and walk across the bottom. To cross a wide stream, they swallow air and paddle across.

The coyotes come out to chase their shadows,
singing their songs to the moon.

The smaller animals hide from the coyotes.

They watch them dance across the hills and
listen to their howls.

Under the ground, the shy skunks line their
den with leaves.

They come up out of their hole at night to
search for food.

The mother opossum carries her babies in her pouch,
looking for a new home.

Sometimes she hangs from a tree limb by her tail.

The porcupine climbs to the top of a tree, looking
for tender bark to eat.

His sharp quills protect him and help keep him safe.

Slowly, the moon sets and the stars fade away.

Now the night animals are ready to sleep.

The sun rises.

The children wake up and start a new day.